MILLION DOLLAR QUESTIONS™

WHAT WOULD YOU DO FOR A MILLION DOLLARS?™

BY
JOHN R. PEAK

authorHOUSE™

1663 LIBERTY DRIVE, SUITE 200
BLOOMINGTON, INDIANA 47403
(800) 839-8640
WWW.AUTHORHOUSE.COM

© 2005 John R. Peak. All Rights Reserved.

No part of this book may be reproduced, stored in a retrieval system, or transmitted by any means without the written permission of the author.

First published by AuthorHouse 10/19/05

ISBN: 1-4208-9757-8 (sc)

Library of Congress Control Number: 2005907064

Printed in the United States of America
Bloomington, Indiana

This book is printed on acid-free paper.

Visit *www.milliondollarquestions.com*
and tell us what you would do for a million dollars.

For my family, friends and especially my loving wife who has always believed in me…

INTRODUCTION

This book was written for one simple reason; all of my friends and family kept telling me that I should write it. I finally decided I would give them what they wanted after a vacation trip to Panama City, Florida. I was sitting on the beach with a friend who is normally skeptical about ideas such as writing books or inventing the "next big thing". However, there is just something about all the expensive beachfront homes and condos that brings up the subject of money and whether we could ever afford to have a house on the beach. The topic came up, as it had many times before, of hypothetical things that we may or may not be willing to do for a million dollars.

It started with a big fat man wearing a Speedo walking down the beach as if he were a hard body and didn't have a care in the world. I posed the first question, "For a million dollars, from this day forward, at the official first day of every summer, you are only allowed to wear a yellow Speedo until the first official day of fall. You can't wear any other type of pants or shorts. Would you do it?" I think his answer was no, but the interesting thing is that "What would you do for a million dollars?™" became the topic of conversation for the next couple of hours. We went back and forth posing question after question (until our wives got sick of it). Once we knew it was time to change the subject, he told me that I should write this book because if we wasted this much time pondering these important questions then surely others would enjoy doing the same.

As you flip through the pages of this book, it may bring new meaning to the old saying "Money Can't Buy Happiness". It may also make you realize that you already have many things in your life that are worth millions to you - your health, your family, your pride and your integrity, just to name a few. I hope that at the very least you simply get a good laugh as you read. If you are one of those people that says "I would do anything for a million dollars", I think you may be humbled a bit.

Before you begin, we should address the ground rules of the game. There are certain assumptions listed on the following page that must be used on all of the situations in this book. As a professional in the field of Million Dollar Questions™, I have run into many people that have tried to come up with some kind of "angle" to get around their obligations and just claim the fictional prize money. Just as in any game, you have to have rules!

I would like to challenge the reader to put this book on your coffee table, take it on your next road trip, or just pull it out the next time you are with friends. I'm betting that you too will waste countless hours pondering what you would do for a million dollars. And when you're done with my questions, you might just start posing your own Million Dollar Questions™.

MILLION DOLLAR
ASSUMPTIONS

1. There is some kind of Godlike enforcement authority that will see to it that you keep up your part of the bargain if you receive the fictional prize money.
2. You can never tell anyone that you received the fictional prize money or why you received it.
3. You have to assume that every situation is possible to do. Some are more "Out There" than others.
4. There is a fictional millionaire who apparently has too much money and too much time on his hands. He will be giving you the fictional prize money to complete these tasks.
5. You cannot give any of the money away to anyone unless specifically mentioned in the given situation.

And, Without Further Ado, Let's Find Out:

What Would You Do For A Million Dollars?™

1. For Men: You will be required to get breast implants. They must be at least a hand full. You have to keep them for life.

2. Picking your nose is bad enough…right? To redeem your prize money, you must eat everything that comes out of your nose. You will have to do this for the next five years.

3. It is halftime at the *Super Bowl*. You have to walk on stage during the halftime show butt naked. The *FCC* will give the television network a free pass for your performance.

4. You must "French Kiss" your mom or your dad for thirty seconds.

5. Getting married to that special someone is a huge moment in every person's life. You will have to ask a woman to marry you in whom you have no interest or attraction and go through with it all the way to the wedding. There must be a minimum of 300 friends and family in attendance. While standing at the Altar, you will be required to tell your new bride or groom in a loud voice that you have made a huge mistake. You must then turn around and walk straight out of the church, get in the limo, and drive away never to return.

6. In this instance, you must buy a twelve-speed bicycle and a helmet. You then have to buy as many white buttoned down short sleeve shirts and black pants as you will need. For the next five years, you have to ride around the neighborhoods of your town knocking on doors and asking if you can tell them about the Gospel.

7. Driving a car or a motorcycle from this day forward is not an option for you. You can only ride a bicycle to get you where you need to go. You are allowed to get rides from friends and family. The exercise will do you some good.

8. Pick out one outfit to wear for a lifetime. You can have as many duplicate pairs of the same clothes so that you don't smell, but you have to wear the same shirt, pants, underwear, shoes, etc. for the rest of your life. You cannot have variation in colors.

9. You will be required to wipe the butt of your worst enemy every time they go to the bathroom for the next five years.

10. Barber shops and hair salons are now off limits. You cannot cut your hair at all for the next five years.

11. For the rest of your life, every time you go into a public bathroom, you have to write your cell number on the wall and above it the words "For a hell of a good time call **Your First And Last Name**". You cannot change your cell number.

12. No more soap operas. No more sitcoms. No more reality TV. You can never watch television again.

13. This might be easy for some and hard for others. You can never drink any alcoholic beverage for the rest of your life.

14. Some men love golf while some women love to shop. Whatever your favorite hobby is, you have to give it up completely from now on.

15. You can never have sexual relations of any kind again. Please refer to *Webster's Dictionary* for the exact definition. We are not using *Bill Clinton's* definition here.

16. Circular saws come in handy on a home renovation project. However, this isn't home renovation but you do have to use a circular saw to cut the finger of your choice off.

17. **For Men:** You must wear a thong for the rest of your life.

18. You are sent to a high-level maximum-security prison where they keep murderers and gang members. You have to spend one full year there and be just another prisoner in the general prison population.

19. This is a personal favorite. You will be placed in a padded cell with no lights, no windows, and plenty of food and water for one solid month with no human contact. There is one added touch. *Vanilla Ice's* famous song *Ice Ice Baby* will be playing continuously.

20. Send an email to your boss with a link to a porn website with a personal message from you that says "I thought you might like this you sick pervert". You must copy the email to his wife. You are not eligible if you are friends with your boss or related to them.

21. Get your haircut exactly like *Vanilla Ice's* hair was when he came out with his debut album. You must keep your hair like this for a period of two years.

22. **For Heterosexuals:** Announce to the world on primetime television that you are coming out as a gay man or lesbian woman and that you are tired of living a lie.

23. Commit a felony that carries a possible prison sentence of twenty years. You can use your prize money to hire a good attorney.

24. For the rest of your life you are not allowed to have a bathroom in your home. Outhouses are permissible.

25. For the rest of your life, anytime you go to the bathroom, you can't look at the toilet seat. You have to just go in the bathroom and plop down without looking. You cannot put toilet paper down. You cannot flush before going. It is purely a "Kamikaze Mission".

26. Also for your lifetime, you must sleep in a coffin with the top closed every night when you go to bed. Breathing will not be a problem. This coffin will be specially designed with plenty of ventilation.

27. **For The Football Fan:** You can never have anything to do with football again. This includes reading the paper, going to the games, watching games on television, listening to games on the radio, watching the highlights on any television channel and betting on the games.

28. Go to a presidential speech where you will position yourself within ten rows of the President. You must then pull out a water pistol that looks identical to a real handgun and wave it in the air while screaming. Once you have screamed for five seconds, turn around and run.

29. Never listen to music again. It doesn't matter if it is the soundtrack at the beginning of your favorite sitcom or the theme to your favorite news program, music is out.

30. You get to choose only one song that you can listen to for the rest of your life. You can never listen to any other music again. You have to listen to this one song at least five times every day. I wonder what song *you* would pick?

31. In this instance you can choose between one of your senses. You can give up the ability to hear, see, taste, smell, or touch. Which sense would you give up?

32. You will be supplied with specially made cologne that smells identical to a horrible smelling fart. You will spray yourself with this every morning for the next five years.

33. This one may seem easier than it really is. You must get a standard typewriter and type, in words, from one to two million. You have two years to complete the task. Your work will be checked and if there is a mistake you have to redo the whole thing.

34. For the next five years, you cannot walk during daylight hours. You must use a wheelchair for the entire day from sunup to sundown. Once it is dark you can walk all you want.

35. You cannot have a home with lights for the next five years. You can only use candlelight. This includes any vacation homes that you might have.

36. Choose any domestic car in the world. Put your seatbelt on and drive down the highway at 70 MPH and turn your wheel sharply. The car has to flip at least once to get the million bucks.

37. Walk at a normal pace down the most populated street in Saudi Arabia with a t-shirt on that says in big letters "I Hate Moslems" in Arabic. You must walk a 200 yard stretch. At the end there will be a helicopter waiting with your prize money ready to air lift you out. There may or may not be heat seeking rocket launchers in the area.

38. Run a paid ad on the screen during halftime at the *Super Bowl* that gives your full name, address, cell number and photo with text that says "I Am A Proud Racist". You can't change your address or cell phone number. You will not have to pay for the ad.

39. Get on the top of a fifty-story building during a severe lightning storm while holding a lighting rod up toward the sky for 30 minutes.

40. For the next five years, you may only wear a *Captain D's* uniform everywhere you go. This includes the hat.

41. Let someone bury you alive in a cemetery. You will be in an oversized coffin with just enough room for you to have food and water. You will be buried for two weeks. Your boss gives you two weeks vacation so your job is not in jeopardy.

42. In this situation, you will be required to have a naked blow up doll with you at all times for the next five years. The doll must be your same sex and you must name it Pat.

43. Let a cobra bite you in the leg. You will have doctors right beside you with the proper anti-venom ready to treat you. The only catch is that once you are bitten you have to listen to *ACDC's* hit song *"Highway to Hell"* all the way through before getting the treatment for the bite. This rock music might properly get your adrenaline pumping to get the venom all the way throughout your body.

44. Sleep in a morgue every night for one year right beside all of the cadavers.

45. **For Men:** Have a permanent tattoo put on your forearm that says "I Like Little Boys".

46. Live as an Amish and adopt all of their traditions for a period of five years.

47. Get in the ring with Mike Tyson and have a boxing match with no gloves. The only way for the fight to end is for one of you to knock the other out cold. You have to look him in the eyes right before the start of the fight and say: "If you think Buster Douglas kicked your ass, wait until I'm done with you".

48. You must get on a 50 foot fishing boat and drive it into the eye of a category five hurricane. You must navigate your own way to safety once you pass through the eye.

49. You must have an outfit made that identically resembles a whitetail deer with a big set of antlers. On opening day of Alabama's deer season, you have to walk out into the woods where there are known hunters in the area and not make a sound. All you can do is walk through the woods as quietly as possible. You can't say a word and you can't make a sound. You must do this from 5:00 AM to 7:00 PM.

50. You have to shoot up heroin one time each day for five days straight. They say that heroin is one of the most addictive drugs there is. Maybe you can prove them wrong.

51. Have a home built on the top of an active landfill. You are required to live there for one year. The home is built for you for free.

52. From now on, every house or car that you rent, lease or own has to be painted completely hot pink.

53. You can never use any phone again. If you need to make a call you have to let someone make the call on your behalf.

54. For the next five years, instead of speaking, you have to write everything instead.

55. You have to have a life sized centerfold picture made of you, butt naked, and mail a signed copy to everyone you know with no explanation of why you had it made or why you sent it. If anyone asks, you can only say "I just thought it was something you needed to see".

56. In this situation you must go into a known *Hell's Angels* bar that is packed with *Hell's Angels* and stand on the bar and yell "How many of you pansy ass bikers think you are going to get out of here without me kicking your ass?" and then sit down and order a pitcher of beer and finish the whole thing. I'm betting on the *Hell's Angels* but if I'm wrong you've just won your prize money.

57. While in mid-flight on a jet airliner, you have to pull a D.B. Cooper and parachute out of the airliner. If you live to tell about it, you will redeem your prize.

58. Elephants are such cute animals. For your big prize you must hold your breath and stick your head in an elephant's butt and leave it there for 30 seconds.

59. For the next five years, you must stop and take one bite out of every tenth road kill you see while driving.

60. There is a 20 acre piece of land that is enclosed by 30 foot high fence. The following animals are put inside: five full-grown tigers, five full-grown lions and five full-grown gorillas. There is plenty of food and water and you must enter the fenced area and live for 30 days. Once you enter the fenced area, you have to stay for the full 30 days.

61. This is a favorite among some of my friends. You must put on a specially made suit that is identical to a seal and go swimming for 20 minutes off the coast of Dyer Island (Known as Shark Alley) in South Africa. This area is home to enormous colonies of fur seals and has one of the largest populations of great white sharks in the world.

62. You must walk up to a known mafia godfather while he is eating spaghetti in his favorite Italian restaurant and slap him across the face and say "How is that for respect?". You can then walk calmly out of the restaurant and redeem your prize money.

63. I hope you like to swim. In this case, you will walk into your local sewer treatment facility, take off all of your clothes, and dive in for a cool swim for one hour.

64. Go out with a storm chaser team in Kansas during a horrible storm. When a tornado is spotted you have to drive straight into the tornado (Remember to buckle your seat belt). Hopefully, you will survive to redeem your prize.

65. You must have your name legally changed to Adolf Hitler and you can never change it. You are required to go by this name from now on.

66. You must drink one gallon of your worst enemy's urine per month for one year. Your enemy will get to watch and make smart comments while you drink.

67. If you think gas prices have gotten bad try this on for size. On your next visit to a dirty gas station, you must walk into the bathroom and lick the entire floor area as well as the toilet seat.

68. For the rest of your life, you can only use newspaper or notebook paper to wipe. You are not allowed to ever use toilet paper or any other soft toilet paper substitute again.

69. Any time you are at home for the next five years you must immediately put on a straight jacket and wear it until you leave your home.

70. You are only allowed to drink *Tab Cola* for the next five years. This means you cannot drink water. However, you will be allowed to drink alcohol during this time.

71. **For Heterosexual Men:** You must live a gay lifestyle for one year. You must conduct your gay lifestyle in the exact way that you have conducted your straight lifestyle.

72. You must get a power drill and drill a five-inch screw into your leg.

73. Have a one on one fight between yourself and a full grown pit bull in an enclosed arena. All you get is a pair of brass knuckles. The last man/dog standing wins.

74. You must drench your body in honey and then lay on top of six fire ant beds that are all in a row for two hours. If the ants calm down you have to move so that they get mad again. Once you are finished, you will receive your prize money while you are being treated for all of your bites.

75. You can never live anywhere that has air conditioning or heat for the rest of your life. You cannot have fans in the house.

76. For the next five years, anytime you have to go to the bathroom you must get someone to put a leash on you and take you outside to go to the bathroom. The person holding the leash must stand there while you use the bathroom.

77. You must put the finger of your choice in boiling water and leave it for 30 Seconds. Once your finger is in the water, you must keep it there until the end of the 30 seconds.

78. We have all been taught to wash our hands before every meal. In this situation you are required to rub both of your hands face down on the nearest toilet seat before every meal. You can't clean the toilet seat before doing this. You just walk in the bathroom and rub away.

79. You will not be allowed to sleep at all for two weeks. If you so much as shut your eyes you lose the prize money.

80. Send an email to all of your friends and family with an attached picture of you butt naked with the message "I just wanted to see if I could get this photo circulated around the internet. Please forward this email to everyone you know".

81. From now on, you have to tell people exactly what you are thinking about them. If your first thought when you see an old friend is how much weight they have gained, you must immediately tell them. I think you get the picture.

82. Every inch of your body must be tattooed all the way up to your neck. You can choose any design you want.

83. You must keep 1,000 live roaches roaming in your home at all times. You cannot use any pesticides and you cannot ever have an exterminator come into your home.

84. Check yourself into a mental institution for the criminally insane and be put in with the general population for one year.

85. You get your one million dollars upfront. The second you get it you must go to a casino and bet the whole million plus $20,000 of your own money on one hand of blackjack.

86. I'm sure you have heard about the guy that went over Niagara Falls in a barrel. In this case, you must go over Niagara Falls in the vessel of your choice. You cannot wear a life jacket.

87. In this situation, every time you ever receive a gift from anyone, right after you open the gift, you have to look them straight in the eyes with a very serious look on your face and say "I hate this". You cannot tell them you are kidding.

88. In this case, you will be getting a million dollars to eat one bite of a human cadaver. You can't throw it up later on. You have to digest it.

89. **For Non-European Women:**
You can never shave your legs again. You cannot wax them or apply any other treatment that would keep the hair from growing.

90. **For Women:** Shave your face like men do for one month and then stop and never shave or wax again. You have to let your facial hair grow naturally for the rest of your life.

91. From now on, wherever you move, you have to immediately contact the local newspaper. You must give them your name, address, photo, and cell number. As long as you live in that town, the newspaper will publish on the front page a picture of you with your name below it saying "Don't call this number unless you want to get your ass kicked". If someone calls you about the ad, your reply has to be "You know where I live bitch." You cannot change any of your contact information.

92. **For Women:** You must be a surrogate mother for five consecutive years. In other words, you will have to have five children that you give away back to back. You can never see the children again once you have had them.

93. In this instance you must create an imaginary friend and take them with you everywhere you go for five years. Every time you speak to someone, at some point you have to turn to your imaginary friend and say something to him or her. Any time you are in a restaurant you must order a meal for your friend as well. You can never let anyone know that you are really kidding.

94. You will be allowed to take as many flying lessons as you want. Once you are comfortable, you have to fly a single engine airplane up 5000 feet above your local airport and turn the engine off and glide into the airport. There must be electrical lines surrounding this airport. It can be any type of single engine plane that you choose but it must have an engine.

95. You will be required to register as a sex offender in every place that you ever live from now on, even though you are not.

96. From this day forward, you will have to wear a cape with every outfit. The cape can be any color you like.

97. You have to have a necklace made and wear it around your neck at all times. The only catch is that instead of a cross you have the numbers 666 (the sign of the devil) hanging on the chain.

98. You have to shoot a bald eagle and have it mounted. You must place it prominently in every place that you ever live with a plaque beside it that has your name, the date of the kill, and an upside down American flag above it.

99. You have to have a large framed picture of you naked prominently displayed in your living room for life.

100. You can never cut your fingernails again.

101. You must have all of your teeth pulled and wear dentures for the rest of your life.

102. You must take your significant other to a "swingers" convention. You will not be participating but your partner will.

103. From the first official day of summer each year until the first official day of fall, you must wear a yellow Speedo wherever you go except for work and special functions such as weddings.

104. You will be required to wear a leisure suit identical to the ones worn by the members of the *Bee Gees* on the *Saturday Night Fever* soundtrack. This includes the gold necklace and medallion. You must wear this everywhere you go for five years.

105. You must have one of your eyes removed and replaced with a glass eye.

106. You will be required to wear a black eye patch like a pirate for the rest of your life. If you are already a pirate you are not eligible.

107. You can never cut your
toenails again.

108. You can never wear deodorant again.

109. You must *Fedex* yourself overnight to another state at least 1,000 miles away. You can create your own container in which you are mailed to your satisfaction and comfort. The only catch is that you will only have twenty-eight hours of oxygen in the container.

110. **For Non Smokers:** Start chain smoking at age 40 for the rest of your life. You must smoke at least one pack a day.

111. Legally adopt fifteen children, all age one, and care for them as their parent for life.

112. You must borrow $1000 from each of your twenty closest friends or family members. You will promise to repay them the next week. Once you have the money, you will never bring it up again. If one of them asks when you will pay them back, all you can say is: "You have plenty of money. Why are you so greedy?"

113. Get in an elevator at the top of a thirty story building and have someone cut the cable. You can put anything inside the elevator that you want to cushion your fall.

114. Go to a poker game that is known to be hosted by the mafia. You have to somehow cheat and let yourself get caught.

115. First, you must sit Indian style with your hands behind you replacing the pins at a bowling alley. A professional bowler will then throw five of his best strikes right at you and you have to remain where you are each time with your hands behind your back.

116. Let someone fly you by helicopter and drop you off in the middle of the Sahara Desert, in the morning at the hottest time of summer. You have no food or water. All you are given is a compass which you will follow east to the nearest town which is 65 miles away. There will be plenty of food and water as well as your prize money waiting for you.

117. You will be enclosed in a room with plenty of ventilation, food and water for one year. You will constantly be visited by a handpicked group of people with a special talent for producing horrible smelling farts. These people will be eating nothing but cheeseburgers, chili dogs and onion rings for the entire year. The only time they will come into your room is when they are ready to leave you a gift behind.

118. Drink a gallon of *Jack Daniels* in an four hour period.

119. The next time you are at your best friend's house, you must log onto the internet on their computer and order "kiddie porn". You must use their home address as the mailing address.

120. You must carry a concrete block around with you wherever you go for the next five years.

121. Have a disc inserted in your lip like the natives do. (You may have seen them on the cover of *National Geographic*.) You must keep your lip that way for one full year. I don't know what you can do about your lip at the end of that year but you'll figure something out.

122. Stand still without moving except to blink for a period of 48 hours. This is much harder than you think. If you don't make it the full 48 hours, you have to give $10,000 of your own money to your worst enemy.

123. You must climb Mount Everest with no oxygen tanks. If you begin the ascent you must go all the way to the top. There is no turning back until you reach the top.

124. You must live in the attic of a home for five years without coming down. You will have your meals brought to you. If you come out of the attic for any reason you forfeit the prize money.

125. You will be closed in a room with fifty rattlesnakes for a 24 hour period and will be provided with plenty of anti-venom kits to take into the room with you. You will also be trained in how to administer the anti-venom to yourself. There will be no furniture in the room so you will be at ground level with the snakes.

126. In this situation you will get to swim 100 yards across the *Zambezi River* in Africa at night. This river is known to be populated with the most dangerous crocodiles in the world.

127. CRIPS and BLOODS are two of the most dangerous rival gangs in Los Angeles. CRIPS wear blue to signify their affiliation while the BLOODS where red. Both gangs have been known to kill rival gang members for wearing the wrong colors in the rival gang's territory.   In this situation, you will be required to wear a completely red outfit with a red bandana. You will then be required to walk, at a normal pace straight through the streets of the CRIPS territory in LA on a Friday night between the hours of 12:00 and 1:00 AM. You will be picked up in a car with bullet proof glass at the end of your journey.

128. You are attending a wedding that you were invited to by a close friend. When the preacher asks if anyone objects to this marriage, you must stand up and say in a loud voice the following: "I object because I am in love with <u>the bride/groom's name</u>". You can never tell them that this is not true. You must always stick with this story from now on.

129. You are getting married to someone whom you genuinely love. When it comes time for you to say your wedding vows, you have to cross your fingers behind your back so that the audience, your future in-laws, and the cameraman can see very well that you have your fingers crossed. You can never tell anyone why you did it.

130. For Religious People: You have to set up a poker table at the Altar in the sanctuary where you worship and deal a poker game with your friends for money while drinking plenty of alcohol. The game will last two hours and you will redeem your prize money at the end of the game.

131. You have to pick two people that you have to be with at all times for the next five years. If one dies, you have to replace them with someone else. The people can be anyone you choose, so pick wisely. The only time that you don't have to be around them is while you are sleeping. You can't choose your significant other as one of your companions.

132. You have to get on prime time television and burn the American flag.

133. First, you have to quit your job. Then you must have all records of any education that you have ever received erased so that you essentially have no record of any education. And finally, anyone that you have ever worked for in your past cannot be used on your resume. From this day forward you cannot get any job through the relationships you have with any friends or relatives. You are also not allowed to have your own business. Now, go find a job.

134. There are many people that go parachuting for adventure or for a hobby. For your prize money, you will parachute out of a plane. The only catch is that you can't pull the ripcord until you are 100 feet above the ground.

135. For Non-Moslems: For the next five years, you must wear a burka like they do in Moslem countries with your face covered anytime you leave your home.

136. You can only take a bath on Sundays for the next five years.

137. For a period of ten years, you have to have a live parrot on your shoulder everywhere you go.

138. For the rest of your life, anytime you have a fart, you have to pull out a lighter, lift your leg and let it go so that everyone around you sees that you are trying to light the gas.

139. You are never allowed to look at your financial information again. The only account you are allowed to look at is the one that your $1,000,000 prize goes into. You have to hand everything else over to a trusted advisor or your spouse.

140. First, you must read the popular book about the *Amityville Horror*. Next, you must watch both the first *Amityville Horror* movie as well as the more recent version. Finally, you will be required to move into the actual house to live for a period of one year.

141. For the next five years, you will have a miniature version of you. You will be allowed to handpick a midget that is with you at all times. Whatever you wear, he or she wears. If you go for a jog, the midget will put on the same outfit as yours and jog with you. You can only tell people that this is your best friend.

142. You are only allowed to wear uniforms for the next five years when you go out in public. You will have a whole closet full of uniforms. Some examples would be: Mechanic, Sea Captain, Bell Hop, Security Guard, and Airline Pilot. If asked why you are wearing a uniform all you can say is "I just felt like being a <u>pilot</u> today." You cannot wear the same uniform two days in a row.

143. Every day for the next five years you have to wear a t-shirt that says "I Think I Just Crapped Myself" in big bold letters. You must wear this shirt at all times.

144. *Mount St. Helens* is a volcano that was recently in the news when it began to erupt. For this situation, you must have a house built near the opening of *Mount St. Helens*. Your new home must be located so that it would be overrun with lava if the volcano erupted. You will be required to live there for five years.

145. This one would be particularly bad for those of you that live in the north. For the next ten years, if the temperature drops below 40 degrees, you have to put on shorts, a short sleeved T-Shirt, and flip flops. This is all you can wear indoors and out.

146. In this situation, you must keep 500 live mosquitoes in your house at all times for one year. You must live in your home just as you do now. You can't use bug spray or any type of bug repellant.

147. For your prize, you must dress up like *Superman* for at least two hours of every day for a period of five years. While you are in your *Superman* outfit you have to go out into the streets of your town offering your protection to the citizens. If you see someone, you must immediately run over to them and ask if you can help them in any way. You must explain to them that you are a superhero and your duty is to protect your community's citizens.

148. You have to be an extra in a porno produced by a major film company. The porno will be distributed widely in stores as well as on the internet.

149. For the rest of your life you have to have a bumper sticker on your car that says "Atheist and Proud Of It"

150. As we all know it has become increasingly dangerous to pick up hitchhikers. This is why you must pick up every hitchhiker you see on the side of the road for the next five years.

151. Have your phone number listed in the yellow pages in the ads for escort services in your town or city. If you move, whatever the largest escort service is in that community, your new phone number gets used in their ad.

152. Dress up in a Big Foot costume and run around in a wooded hunting preserve during hunting season for one full day. You cannot make any sounds other than the one similar to *Chewbacca* in *Star Wars*.

153. This one may bring some unwanted calls. You must write your name and cell phone number on every dollar bill that goes through your hands with the word "Bi-Curious" written beside it. You cannot change your cell number. You must do this for a period of one year.

154. You have to be a mime for one year. This means all the time you must be dressed up in full mime gear and you cannot speak.

155. You have to have a swastika tattooed on your forearm. It must be at least 2" X 2" but it can be larger if you like. You can never have it removed.

156. You have to get your hair cut exactly like *Billy Ray Cyrus* when his *Achy Breaky Heart* song was popular. You must keep it that way for two years.

157. Tell everyone you know about your best friend's deepest darkest secret. It must be a secret that would devastate your best friend if others knew.

158. If you have a best friend that has cheated on their spouse or significant other, you have to tell on them. You can only tell your friend that it was bothering you and you felt it was your duty to tell the truth.

159. You can never have any pictures of your friends or family again. You have to get rid of all your current pictures.

160. You can never watch a movie again.

161. You can never use a stove or microwave again to cook your meals. You cannot have someone else do it for you.

162. You can never use fire again.

163. You can never use a dishwasher or washer/dryer again.

164. You can never wear shoes again.

165. Legally have your name changed to a two word Indian name with an adjective and animal name together. Examples would be Soaring Eagle, Howling Wolf, and Growling Bear.

166. Everywhere you live from now on can only have 5 Foot ceilings.

167. You cannot laugh for the next year.

168. You can only go to the doctor or the emergency room a total of three visits in a five year period. The only exception is for pregnant women. The visits having to do with the pregnancy will not count against the allowed three visits. You get your prize money upfront on this one, so if you agree, it doesn't matter what occurs, you only get the three visits.

169. You will have a "drill sergeant" assigned to you for the next five years. This drill sergeant can show up any time he wants. When he shows up he gets right in your face and yells, screams and cusses you about how you screwed up on something. It will be just like you are going through basic training except you are a civilian. You could be having dinner with your family at a restaurant and in comes your personal drill sergeant calling you a "stupid worthless maggot" right there in public. You must always just sit there and take it like a man.

170. At all times for the next two years, you have to keep a dead fish in every room of your home. Every month you can replace them with a new dead fish in each room. You must live in your home just as you do now for this two year period.

171. For Men: Wear women's underwear, bras, and lingerie all the time for the next five years.

172. Have the quote "Atkins Approved" branded on your butt.

173. You must flip the switch at an execution that you know nothing about. In other words, you know nothing about why the person is being executed. You just walk in, flip the switch, walk out and claim your money.

174. You have to make advances towards your best friend's significant other. You cannot tell your best friend about it and you cannot tell his or her significant other anything about why you are doing it. They must think it is for real.

175. For one year, every time you have to go to the bathroom you have to do it in your pants and you can't clean up until 7:00 PM every night. Yes, this includes number one and number two.

176. You must leave the country without telling any of your friends or family and live abroad for one year. You cannot make contact with any of them for the full year. After your year is up, you return to the prize money and your friends and family. Maybe they'll forgive you but you can never tell them why you really did it.

177. Spray paint your name and phone number on the Washington Monument. You can't change your phone number. You will be immune from prosecution.

178. This one may test you as a human. Vandalize the Vietnam Veterans Memorial with spray paint. It must be where the names of the soldiers that died for our country are written.

179. Legally change your name to Osama bin Laden. You can never change it.

180. Have a tracking device attached to your ankle just like the ones they put on people that are under house arrest. A website will be established where people can go to see where you are at any given time. Everyone you talk to has to be given the address of the website and told how it works. This device will be attached for five years.

181. Get your own personal dietician to help you gain 100 lbs. Once you have gained the weight you get the prize. You can then lose it.

182. Never buy or pay for any kind of insurance again. This includes health insurance.

183. Grow your own food from now on. If you like meat, you can have all the cows and chickens you want.

184. From now on, every retarded or handicapped person you see, you have to point and laugh so that they know you are pointing at them.

185. You have to tell five bold faced lies a day to a friend or family member. These cannot be "white lies". They must be lies with consequences.

186. You have to make fun of one person every day that is less fortunate than you. You have to explain to them why you have a better situation than they do in life.

187. Never celebrate your
birthday again.

188. Never celebrate
any holiday again.

189. You can only go outside when it's raining for the next ten years.

190. For Dog Lovers: Give your dog away. You must have had the dog for at least three years to be eligible. You can never get your dog back and you can never see them again.

191. There is a one acre minefield that contains ten mines. You have to walk from one corner to the other to redeem your prize money.

192. You must go to the Daytona 500 and sit in the general admission "cheap seats". It is required that you walk around in this area for the entire race while wearing a shirt that says in bold letters "Dale Earnhardt Sucked Anyway!" with the number 3 written backwards below the writing.

193. For Men: I hope you like baseball. In this situation you will have to stand at home plate in a major league stadium. Your legs will be spread with your hands behind your back. Randy Johnson (The Big Unit) will proceed to throw three of his fastest strikes at the strike zone, which happens to be your unit.

194. You have to hang the American Flag upside down from the front porch of your home wherever you live from now on.

195. You can never have any contact with your father or mother on father's/mother's day again.

196. Never use a computer or the internet again. This includes your job. You may have to get a job that doesn't require a computer.

197. Never take any over the counter medications again.

198. Never lock your doors or windows in your home or car again. You are also not allowed to have alarms.

199. Stay underwater until you pass out. There will be doctors present to revive you but not until you physically pass out.

200. Only brush your teeth once a week for the next five years.

201. Vandalize the Mona Lisa. You will have full immunity from prosecution.

202. Give up the right to bear arms.

203. Give up your
due process rights.

204. Change your will so that everything you own is given to your worst enemy upon your death. Your wife, children, family, and friends get nothing. The will can never be changed again.

205. You must learn a new language and once learned, you get your prize money and you can never speak your native language again.

206. Live with your parents for the rest of your life. You have to sleep in the bed with them at least five days of the week.

207. You must learn sign language and only use this type of communication for the next five years.

208. You must have a professionally made sign that runs across the windshield of any car you drive from now on that says "69 Party Time".

209. Go on a one week trip to Japan. The whole trip you must wear a t-shirt with a picture of the World War II Hiroshima nuclear explosion with the words in Japanese below the picture: "Hiroshima 1945", as if it were a concert.

210. You are stranded on a desert island, which is ten square miles wide. You have plenty of food and water. This is all you have with you besides the clothes on your back. You will remain on the island for two years with no human contact. A helicopter will pick you up and take you home at the two-year mark and you will be given your prize money at that time. There is just one small problem. The island is inhabited by ten man-eating tigers.

211. They say all that really matters is family. For the next five years, you will not be allowed to speak to any of your immediate family members.

Dear Reader: I would love to hear your ideas on what you would do for a million dollars. Please visit *www.milliondollarquestions.com* to give us your ideas and feedback. We may include your ideas in future *Million Dollar Questions™* releases.
You can also mail correspondence to:
John R. Peak
P.O. Box 1062
Columbus, GA 31902

Printed in the United States
40687LVS00001B/61-69